LEGAL ISSUES AROUND NFTS AND WAY FORWARD

VOLUME 2, ISSUE 1 OF BRILLOPEDIA

UTKARSH KUMAR

ISBN 979-888629208-4

Contents

Preface

"Start writing, no matter what. The water does not flow until the faucet is turned on".

-Louis L'Amour

Hundreds of students and professors are contributing their work to Brillopedia, we are here to provide ample information about Law and Contemporary issues. Our aim is to provide a platform for today's generation to express their views and ideas on law and contemporary law.

Author

Utkarsh Kumar

Publication

This research paper is published in volume 2, issue 1 of Brillopedia

CHAPTER ONE

Abstract

Non fungible tokens (also known as NFTs) are a relatively new concept that has taken the digital market by storm. A digital token system that first surfaced in early 2020 has now grown into a thriving billion-dollar enterprise.As we move closer to 2021, the drumbeat of the cryptocurrency and broader digital asset industries continues, and non-fungible tokens have become more popular as a result (NFTs). As a new technology, it also has a grey area linked with it: legal concerns, activities that haven't yet evolved to deal with the situation, buyers and sellers who haven't yet grasped the future elements, and people's capacity to exploit the loopholes around it. In recent months, sales of non-fungible tokens (NFTs) have exploded. Businesses in a variety of industries have issued NFTs to promote brand awareness, capitalise on metaverse gaming prospects, and compensate artists for their creative production. The ease with which these tokens can be copied and their copyrights infringed is one of their most problematic features. Every new technological advancement has a more severe adverse consequence. As a result of NFT and cryptocurrency minting, such an influence can be found in the environment

CHAPTER TWO

Introduction

We are faced with the much-associated risk of copyrights in today's digital environment, when anything and everything may be gotten online. With the use of NFTs, even non-abstract things on the digital interface like digital art, a tweet, or a GIF may be marketed. With the rise of cryptocurrencies, where even currency was digitalized and sold, it wasn't difficult to turn digital art into the next virtual token. Some of them have fetched astronomical sums of money; for example, an NFT by Beeple, a digital artist, was auctioned for 69.3 million USD[1]. In addition, creators are using NFTs to come up with new ways to monetize digital creative works and other experiences, like the Kings of Leon did when they released their new album as a limited edition NFT, with six NFTs offering lifetime tickets to front row seats at the band's gigs. Blockchains underpin the use of NFTs for digital creative creations. Blockchains are immutable digital ledgers that record transactions in "blocks" of computer code that are time stamped and linked together, indicating a digital asset's provenance[2].

[1] Scott Reyburn, JPG File Sells for $69 Million, as 'NFT Mania' Gathers Pace Nytimes.com (2021), https://www.nytimes.com/2021/03/11/arts/design/nft-auction-christies-beeple.html#:~:text=After%20a%20flurry%20of%20more,for%20%2469.3%20million%20 with%20 fees.

[2] https://www.whitecase.com/publications/alert/rise-nfts-opportunities-and-legal-issues

CHAPTER THREE

What are NFTs?

Non-fungible Tokens, or NFTs, are digital tokens that can be used to buy or sell any digital item, such as a GIF, a tweet, or art. It's comparable to how an art curator selects and owns one-of-a-kind art treasures that they own and have in their hands.

The greater the demand for a work of art, the higher its value will be. As a result, this mechanism is based on the demand hypothesis. NFTs are tokens in the Ethereumblockchain, a popular blockchain network. The technology is the same as that utilised in cryptocurrency.

NFTs provide a technique to establish a "original" or "genuine" version of easily replicated digital content or assets. We prefer to think of NFTs as blockchain-based digital trading cards. For example, an e-sports player might create an NFT of their character's digital "skin" or costume when they won a gaming championship. The "original" web source code was just generated and auctioned by the inventor of the internet[1].

They are purchased and sold online on specific platforms such as OpenSea, a well-known NFT platform. The buyer obtains a certificate of ownership once the price is paid online using bitcoins. The name on the certificate of ownership switches from the seller to the buyer, indicating that the token has changed hands[2].

Some NFTs have "smart contracts," which specify how content interactions might take place, for example. The coding is stored on the blockchain as part of the token and executes automatically when certain conditions occur. For example, the smart contract could be set up so that access to the underlying digital asset is only allowed when payment is received, or so that the digital asset's original developer is paid anytime the NFT is sold[3].

[1] https://www.osborneclarke.com/insights/what-are-legal-issues-around-nfts

[2] https://ijclp.com/legal-issues-surrounding-nfts/

[3] https://www.osborneclarke.com/insights/what-are-legal-issues-around-nfts

CHAPTER FOUR

Legal problems associated to NFTs

NFTs are a relatively new technological notion that has swept the internet. NFTs, on the other hand, come with a few drawbacks.NFTs are still in their infancy and have a bleak future ahead of them. Putting a substantial sum of money into such a new technology is extremely bold and financially dangerous.Furthermore, because demand determines pricing, the cost of an NFT is determined by how much the piece signifies to the seller. They are not constrained by economic considerations.

Despite rumours that NFTs will be officially regulated under the Markets in Crypto-Assets Regulation (MiCAR), they are still unregulated. Existing laws and regulations will still apply, and any company issuing, dealing, or exchanging NFTs would have to consider a number of commercial and legal considerations.

- Intellectual Property Rights

The underlying intellectual property rights are not held by the author or owner of an NFT simply because it is built to display an underlying work of art. To gain the right to duplicate the original work, NFT holders must secure a licence of these underlying rights from people who created it. Those who control such rights may want to grant a licence along with other restrictions on how and by what means an NFT can be utilised.

People from various walks of life participate in the NFT market, and many are unaware of the legal limits that apply to copyrighted content, potentially exposing them to infringement penalty. For example, an NFT purchaser may believe that he has purchased the underlying art that is linked with the NFT; however, the copyright owner is the original author, who retains the exclusive right to copy, distribute, modify, publicly perform, and publicly display the art (unless specifically granted to someone else). Alternatively, the token and the right to use the copyrighted art connected with the NFT are often solely given to the purchaser of the NFT for personal use. Under a variety of legal grounds, a purchaser who believes the rights connected with the underlying work were misrepresented and who sees a loss in value could bring litigation against the NFT seller[1].

- Data Hosting and storage

Typically, an NFT and the digital object it represents are kept distinct. The NFT is a digital asset that is kept on the blockchain and provides information about its location. The digital asset is linked to the NFT via a connection. The link will break if the digital asset is erased or the server hosting it fails or otherwise goes offline, and the NFT that remains will be worthless because it will no longer be associated with the digital asset and there will be no way to back it up. Because the NFT is one-of-a-kind and cannot be replicated, the purchaser of the NFT may be without remedy. This might result in business interruptions, regulatory record-keeping infractions, and other issues depending on how the NFT is used.

- Royalties

It is feasible to distribute money to pay royalties to the creator by using smart contracts written into the code of NFTs. A seller may be compensated at the time their work of art is sold. One criterion is to resell the work. The same platform must be used to resell an NFT. This is the most important requirement for auto-resale royalty payments to occur. It is feasible to distribute money to pay royalties to the creator by using smart contracts written into the code of NFTs. A seller may be compensated at the time their work of art is sold. One criterion is to resell the work. The same platform must be used to resell an NFT. This is the most important requirement for auto-resale royalty payments to occur[2]. However, until the NFT is resold using the same platform, these automated resale royalty payments may not be made. Because US law does not recognise resale rights for creative works, there is no legal redress for unpaid resale royalties in the United States, as it does in about 70 other jurisdictions, including the United Kingdom and the European Union.

- Anti-Money Laundering

Because of their novel and unexplored nature, NFT market participants should not believe that they are immune to regulation. NFTs prompted the formation of separate statutes, one of which is a recent class-action lawsuit. Global restrictions on art, digital assets, and antiquities have recently been expanded, particularly in terms of anti-money laundering (AML)[3].

NFT fractions have been categorised as securities by the SEC in the United States, and AML regulatory organisations are taking notice as well. That is one illustration. Market NFT actors active in the purchase and sale of these tokens, such as art dealers and brokers, would be prepared to assess what could be at stake while navigating these new waters, given the significant penalty of non-compliance[4].

- Contractual

To "mint" NFTs, issuers frequently hire a third-party technology vendor. The "minting" agreement must clearly specify the scope of the provider's responsibilities and provide assurances that intellectual property and confidential information will be adequately protected (particularly as NFT projects can be commercially sensitive).

To "mint" NFTs, crypto funds will be required, hence organisations should consider purchasing an enterprise-grade crypto wallet. To ensure effective protection in the event of loss or misuse of crypto assets in the wallet, thorough vendor due diligence will be required[5].

The terms under which NFTs are offered for sale to purchasers must be carefully defined, in addition to any agreements with technological partners. These will most likely take the form of "conventional" legal conditions that the buyer accepts at the point of sale, possibly combined with a smart contract that automates some elements. They'll have to be written in accordance with local consumer protection laws, which could provide buyers legal recourse in their native country.

- Data protection regulations

If we consider the EU, as GDPR acknowledges, there is at least one legal individual against whom data subjects can assert their rights in connection to every private data point (for example, rectifying or eliminating personal information).A similar regulation exists in the United States, which allows people to completely remove their personal information on occasion. Some data protection legislation, such as the California Consumer Privacy Act or the EU General Data Protection Regulation's requirements, allow for this.

However, due to some impediments that a blockchain may impose, users may be unable to exercise their privilege. It does not need users to reveal their identities. As a result, data subjects have a difficult time exercising their rights. Some data protection rules may be violated by non-fungible tokens that include private data[6].

[1]   https://www.whitecase.com/publications/alert/rise-nfts-opportunities-and-legal-issues

[2] https://opengeekslab.com/blog/legal-issues-nfts/

[3] https://opengeekslab.com/blog/legal-issues-nfts/

[4] https://opengeekslab.com/blog/legal-issues-nfts/

[5]   https://www.osborneclarke.com/insights/what-are-legal-issues-around-nfts

[6] https://opengeekslab.com/blog/legal-issues-nfts/

CHAPTER FIVE

Laws in India governing sale and purchase of NFTs

The Supreme Court overturned the RBI circular prohibiting trading with cryptocurrencies in Internet and Mobile Association of India v. RBI.

The Copyright Act of 1957[1] addresses one of the concerns surrounding copyright. It stipulates that copyrights are explicitly transferred from the seller to the buyer. As a result, the governing sales contract determines the parties' rights and the scope of those rights in an NFT sale[2].

It can also be governed by the Contract Act[3], which lays out the rules for making a sale and purchase agreement. It governs the owner's obligations and the purchaser's rights, and so can be used to regulate the circulation of NFTs. However, under Smart Contracts, the consideration is a cryptocurrency, which raises the issue of the transaction's legitimacy once more.

NFTs can be considered assets under the SRCA[4], making them subject to the Securities Act's regulations. If they are viewed as derivatives, their legality is once again called into doubt. Only derivatives sold on recognised markets or stock exchanges are legitimised by the Act. Market platforms for non-financial-transactions (NFTs) that are not authorised by law cannot be held in the same position.

Because the vast majority of cryptocurrencies are created outside of India, a provider may be subject to additional rules.

[1] Copyright Act, 18 (1957)

[2] SujataChaudhri, NFT regulations in India Law.asia (2021), https://law.asia/nft-regulations-india/#:~:text=Once%20the%20 rights%20are%20 assigned,by%20the%20 government%20 sales%20contract (last visited Jan 23, 2022).

[3] Indian Contract Act, 10 (1872)
[4] Securities Contract (Regulation) Act, 1956 (SCRA)

CHAPTER SIX

Way Forward

There have been discussions about transitioning from blockchain to Casper, a more environmentally friendly technology. It will use a proof of stake algorithm instead of a proof of work algorithm. It is expected to reduce carbon emissions by a large amount, according to researchers. Currently, however, the energy usage of Bitcoin and Ethereum technologies exceeds that of countries such as Mexico, Saudi Arabia, and even Italy in a single year. According to a report by Reuters, NFT sales and purchases totaled 2.5 billion USD in the first half of 2020[1]. The future market for NFTs is uncertain because it is the first of its kind.

NFTs are quickly becoming one of the most rapidly growing and blooming new-age sectors in crypto, and acceptability is growing this year. Non-fungible Tokens (NFTs) were the most important issue in the blockchain world in 2021. Utility, gaming, and gaining admission to extremely elite and desirable communities would be the focus of NFTs. It's also well-established in the music industry, with a number of musicians publishing NFT-formatted works.

In 2022, with NFTs in gaming starting to take off in a big way, there will be a huge increase. Dolce &Gabbana and Nike, for example, have created their own NFTs for clothing and footwear. And the metaverse concept, which was championed by Facebook, Microsoft, and Nvidia this year, opens up a slew of potential NFT use cases.

NFTs are gaining popularity and will soon become an integral component of popular culture. By facilitating the sale of digital assets and giving digital artists with a range of monetization options, NFTs are revolutionising the arts, music, and sports industries. In the live entertainment industry, the most essential area for NFTs is fan involvement. Many artists, for instance, have begun to create and sell NFT artwork to their fans[2].

Without a doubt, NFTs are revolutionising the arts, music, and sports industries by easing the sale of digital assets and providing digital artists with a variety of monetization choices. NFT will continue to be a hot subject in 2022, disrupting industries like as gaming, art, and creativity, among others. MANA, AXS, SAND, and other top NFT coins will continue to gain traction. And the metaverse notion, which was championed this year by Facebook, Microsoft, and Nvidia, throws up a slew of possible NFT use cases.

[1] Dragos.I. Musan, "NFT-finance Leveraging Non-Fungible Tokens",

[2] https://www.cnbctv18.com/cryptocurrency/nft-a-disruptor-in-crypto-space-in-2021-and-the-way-forward-12184602.htm

Conclusion

The amount of NFT sales appears to be heading for the stars, putting regulatory agencies in a rush to come up with any meaningful standards for their supervision. NFTs, on the other hand, allow complete anonymity, making them an ideal platform for money laundering and illegal privacy. Virtual currency exchanges and custodial wallet providers are now included in the European Union's anti-money laundering rules. The European Commission recommended that crypto-assets be regulated under the Markets in Crypto-assets Regulation, which would apply to NFTs in certain circumstances.

Several investors have labelled the bitcoin sector as a bubble right now. However, it will be intriguing to observe if NFTs represent the art market's future or a much-hyped bubble. Notably, NFTs have transformed hitherto unknown methods, identities, and ways of monetizing assets. This market, which is still in its infancy, continues to grow, despite the legal and environmental challenges that surround it.